EARLY-ELEMENTARY PIANO SOLOS

COMPOSER SHOWCASE
HAL LEONARD
STUDENT PIANO LIBRARY

Jazz Prelims

FIVE-FINGER PIANO SOLOS IN VARIOUS JAZZ STYLES

BY BILL BOYD

CONTENTS

Editor: Barbara Kreader

ISBN 978-0-7935-4522-3

HAL•LEONARD®
CORPORATION
7777 W. BLUEMOUND RD. P.O. BOX 13819 MILWAUKEE, WI 53213

Copyright © 1995 by HAL LEONARD CORPORATION
International Copyright Secured All Rights Reserved

Visit Hal Leonard Online at
www.halleonard.com

TO THE STUDENT

This book contains pieces which are written in the jazz, rock, and pop styles. For example, in the songs **Bass Guitar Blues** and **Bass Guitar Rock**, you will be playing the bass part and imitating the sound of the bass guitar. Listen carefully as you play the duets and you will hear many familiar jazz sounds.

Know your part thoroughly before playing with your teacher. Accurate note and rhythm playing is very important.

Good luck and enjoy your first experience with jazz.

TO THE TEACHER

Duets develop a strong sense of rhythm so essential to good jazz playing. While each melody has a jazz flavor and will stand on its own as a solo, the student will hear many authentic jazz sounds in the accompaniment parts.

Most of the selections are in the MIDDLE C POSITION with an occasional flat. Two pieces move the hand position slightly to provide more note-reading experiences.

The last two duets contain eighth-notes. The student will listen as the teacher plays uneven swing eighth-notes and then imitate the exact notes and rhythm pattern.

Blues Parade

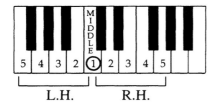

By Bill Boyd

Duet Part (Student plays one octave higher than written.)

A Minor Effort

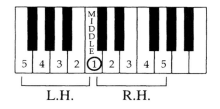

By Bill Boyd

Jazz Waltz

Duet Part (Student plays one octave higher than written.)

Jazz Waltz

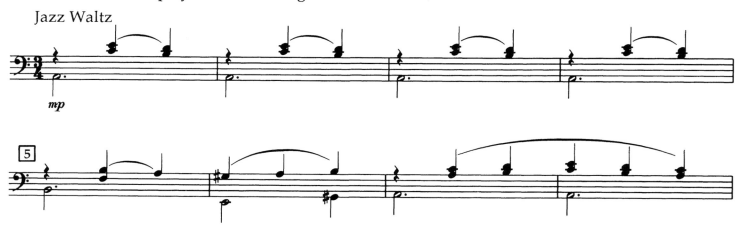

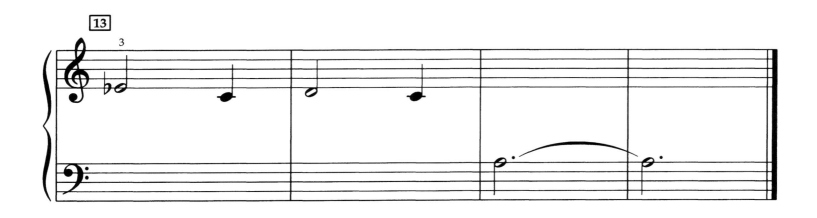

Bass Guitar Blues

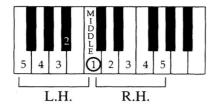

L.H.   R.H.

By Bill Boyd

With a beat

Duet Part (Student plays one octave lower than written.)

With a beat

Love Theme For A TV Series

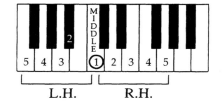

By Bill Boyd

Slow Rock Ballad

Duet Part (Student plays one octave higher than written.)

Slow Rock Ballad

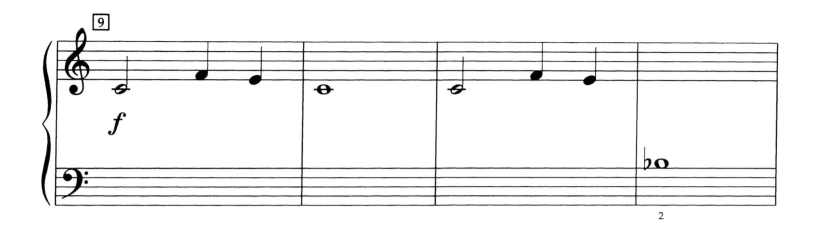

Triple Play

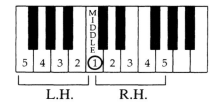

By Bill Boyd

Moderately

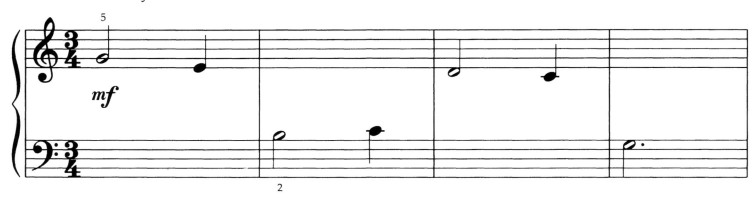

Duet Part (Student plays one octave higher than written.)

Moderately

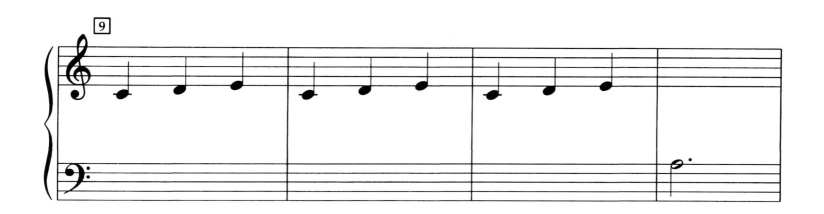

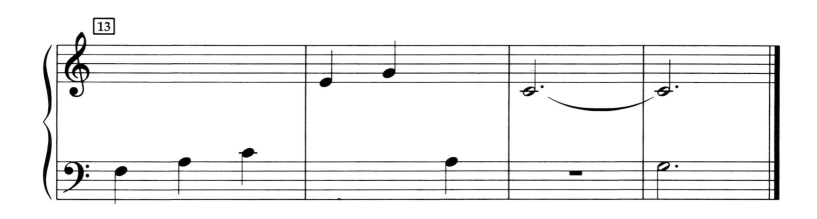

Smooth Groove

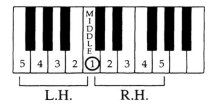

By Bill Boyd

In a smooth Jazz groove

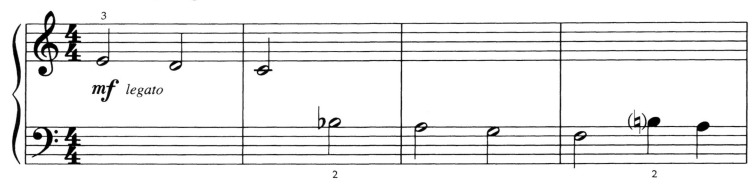

Duet Part

In a smooth Jazz groove

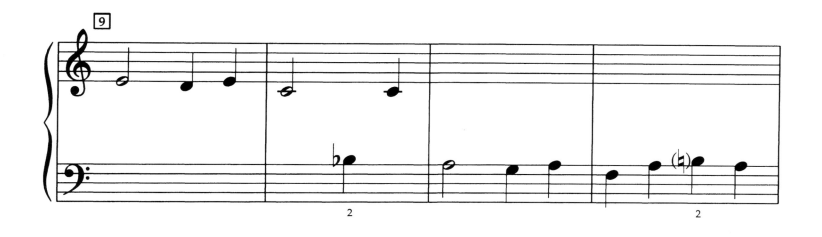

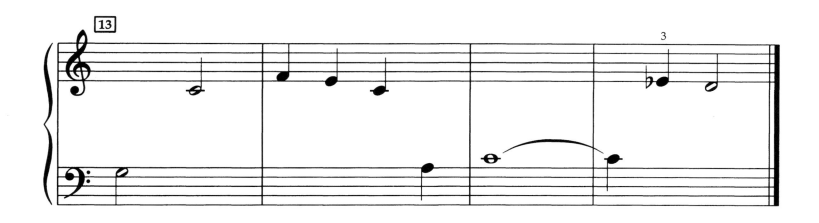

Tick Tock The Jazz Clock

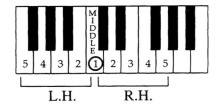

By Bill Boyd

With a steady beat like the tick of a clock

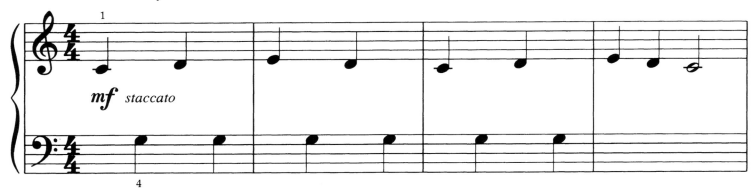

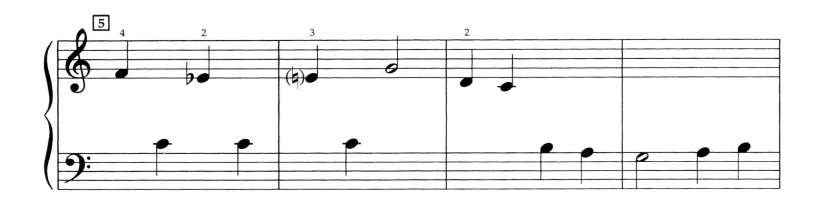

Duet Part

Jazz Time

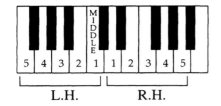

By Bill Boyd

Moderately

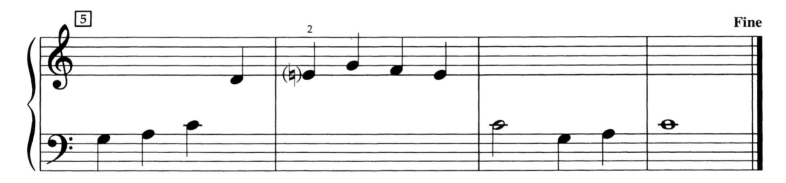

Duet Part (Student plays one octave higher than written.)

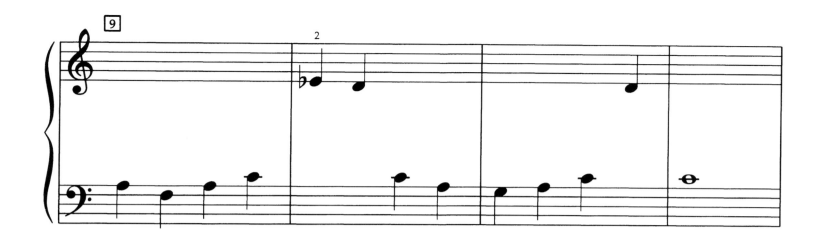

D.C. al Fine

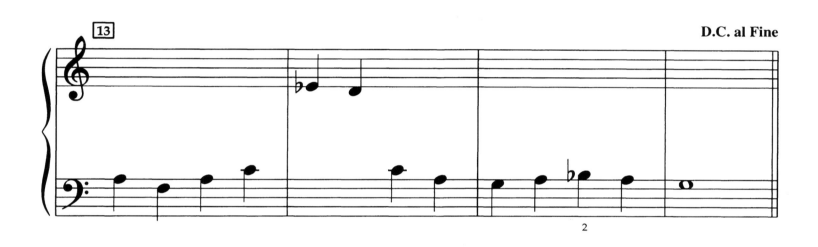

D.C. al Coda

CODA

Take A Rest

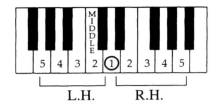

By Bill Boyd

Moderately, with a steady beat

Duet Part (Student plays one octave higher than written.)

Moderately, with a steady beat

Bass Guitar Rock

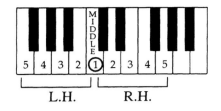

By Bill Boyd

Moderately, with a steady Rock beat

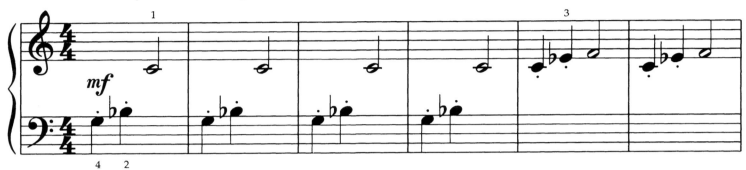

Duet Part (Student plays one octave lower than written.)

Moderately, with a steady Rock beat (♩♩ = ♩♩)

Follow the Leader

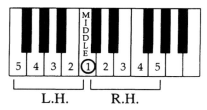

By Bill Boyd

Listen to the eighth notes as played by your teacher in measure one.
Play your eighth notes exactly as you heard them.

Steady Swing

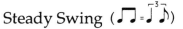

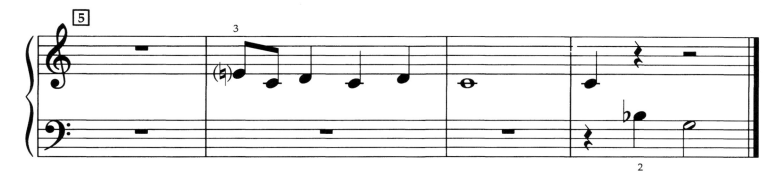

Duet Part (Student plays one octave higher than written.)

Steady Swing

Imitation

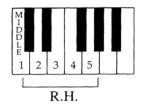

R.H.

By Bill Boyd

Imitate the way your teacher plays the eighth notes.

Moderate Swing

Duet Part (Student plays one octave higher than written.)

Moderate Swing